The Seventh Distinction

The Path to Personal Mastery, Leadership & Peak Performance

The Seventh Distinction
The Path to Personal Mastery, Leadership & Peak Performance

by
Luis E. Romero

Copyright © 2012 by Luis E. Romero.
All rights reserved. No part of this book may be reproduced, stored, scanned, or distributed in any printed or electronic form without the prior written permission of the publisher.

Image of the number seven on cover used under license from Shutterstock.com.

First Edition: December 2012.
Minor edits and cover redesign: September 2016.
Minor edits: June 2020.

Published by
Luis Romero International LLC, Miami, Florida.
Visit our website at leromero.com.

ISBN: 978-0-9886926-0-2 (Paperback)
ISBN: 978-0-9886926-1-9 (Hardback)
Library of Congress Control Number: 2012922753

Printed in the United States of America

To my loving and beloved wife, Katherine. You are so intelligent, hardworking, and beautiful. Thank you for helping me see my true self so I can progressively break free from my ego. Thank you for helping me do so every single day, especially when I need it most.

CONTENTS

INTRODUCTION 1

CHAPTER ONE 11
Complication vs. Complexity:
The Rise of Simplicity

CHAPTER TWO 19
Understanding vs. Learning:
The Rise of Evolution

CHAPTER THREE 33
Management vs. Influence:
The Rise of Leadership

CHAPTER FOUR 45
Talent vs. Personality:
The Rise of Competency

CHAPTER FIVE 55
Ambition vs. Mission:
The Rise of Vision

CHAPTER SIX 67
Obligation vs. Conviction:
The Rise of Principle

CONTENTS

CHAPTER SEVEN 75
Ego vs. Self:
The Rise of Consciousness

REFERENCES 89

INDEX 93

INTRODUCTION

The Parable of the Room

A successful professional was exhausted and strained by his many duties. After much self-debate, he decided to go and see a spiritual master who lived nearby. Once there, he was asked by the master to sit down and take a detailed look at the room. The man assumed he would be quizzed about the room's contents so he tried to memorize as many details as possible. The master let him be. After a while, the master requested him to close his eyes and then probed, "Are your eyes fully closed?" The man, somewhat excited, answered, "Yes." Then, the master examined, "What do you see?" The man, a little more excited, responded, "I see the room." So, the master told him, "That's your problem." The man, confused, could not help but open his eyes and inquired, "What do you mean?" The master replied, "You let the outside world define your inner world—so much so, in fact, that when you close your eyes, you still see the outside. You always know where you are, but you hardly know who you are. You will always adapt well, but you are here because you forgot who you are." "What should I do?" the man asked. The master responded, "From now on, when you close your eyes, see beyond the imprint from the outside. That will be your new beginning."

THE SEVENTH DISTINCTION

"The Parable of the Room" summarizes the purpose of this book, which is to help you go through a gradually introspective process of personal and professional development. A process that starts with your ability to see within yourself.

This introduction, in turn, relates the origin of the seven distinctions that comprise the body of this book, and encompass the most valuable lessons from my own journey of personal and professional development. Let us begin.

From the Comfort Zone to Restlessness

Ever since I was a kid, I was interested in acquiring knowledge—it amazed me, entertained me, and boosted my ego. However, after I graduated from college, I started to realize that, despite all the knowledge that I had gained, I could not stop the development of a profoundly anxious, apprehensive, and obsessive me.

Although I had initiated my professional life with a job sought after by many, as time passed, I gradually started to feel like a hostage of mainstream society. The successful adaptations I had made to the world around me were not contributing to my general wellbeing. The way I experienced life was changing profoundly.

Introduction

For example, I had always been fascinated by technology; yet I started to feel hypnotized and enslaved by it. Likewise, I used to be inspired by religion; however, as I started to become an adult in the real world, I felt dangerously stifled by its dogmas. Similarly, I had always been intellectually stimulated by science; yet, ever more frequently, I unconsciously related to it as if it were a religion, thus feeling again dangerously stifled. In conclusion, I started to feel that my old ways were causing me discomfort.

I also realized that the more I became involved in mainstream society, the more difficult it was for me to escape my almost permanent feelings of anxiety, apprehension, and obsession. I regularly tried to compensate for such feelings by exercising, vacationing, and socializing, but I never really let go. I was feeling restless and needed to learn to live my life in a different way.

From Knowledge to Self-Knowledge

It was not until after much personal struggle, devoted search, and blissful assistance from other people, that I turned to my inner self for guidance. It was then that I felt that my studies and expertise in several fields had real value. I started to use them to figure out myself, rather than let them dictate who I was.

THE SEVENTH DISTINCTION

I realized that there is a significant difference between who I am and what I know, no matter how closely related both are. Such a distinction motivated me to pursue self-knowledge—the very kind of knowledge I was missing but naïvely pretended to have on the basis of my intellectualized ego. This is how I became introduced to the art and science of personal mastery—the pursuit of my inner truth so that no one nor anything, especially my ego, can fool me.

This is how, after a life based upon the pursuit of perfection, it dawned on me that such a pursuit is just madness—especially because my concept of perfection negated all that I am as a human being. This became the beginning of experiencing my emotions, feelings, thoughts, and actions in an honest way. A way that allowed me to acknowledge and experience my flaws as part of my imperfect but very powerful self.

I also started to replace a convoluted and anxious sense of certainty with a more fluid sense of purpose. One that included uncertainty as an inexorable component of reality, which allowed me, for the first time, to focus on my goals without feeling so much anguish.

Introduction

From the Pursuit of Success to the Pursuit of Self-Realization

From this new vantage point, success took on a whole different meaning. The rat race was no longer my path and the expectations of others were no longer my fuel. Traditional objectives such as recognition and money remained present, but they were now a means to an end, not the end itself. The ultimate goal now was to rediscover myself honestly so I could lead a more fulfilling life.

This was the beginning of my path toward personal mastery—an intense, messy, sometimes almost fatal battle against my ego in pursuit of the Promised Land within myself. As I became initiated on this path, I started to exert a better influence on my family, my clients, and those with whom I share my life. This was also my introduction to the notion of peak performance, a concept that revolves around achieving what is right for me rather than what others expect me to achieve.

Self-realization turned out to be at the core of this new approach to success. I finally learned that, without self-realization, the laurels of success are made of thorns.

From Knowledge to Wisdom

As I sought a new, more fulfilling path, I

THE SEVENTH DISTINCTION

realized that knowledge gave me tools, whereas self-knowledge gave me wisdom. It is such wisdom that allowed me to put the knowledge I had acquired in context and into perspective, so that it would finally serve my general well-being rather than just boost my ego. Here are some examples.

When I first became highly proficient in computer applications, my professional productivity increased exponentially. Yet, when I first experienced the knockout impact of Jesus' statement, "The Truth shall set you free," I reassessed myself in a way that changed my professional path forever. In this example, knowledge made me productive, while wisdom led me to be productive at something that I really loved.

Similarly, when I first understood Einstein's theories of relativity, I felt very intelligent. Yet I felt unmasked when I first read Osho's claim that the ego is "subtle (…) It comes like a whisper (…) Once it has taken possession of you, then it is very difficult [to break free from it]."[1] In this example, knowledge boosted my ego, while wisdom helped me see my ego at work so I could tame it and manage it.

Finally, when I first became proficient in systems thinking, I felt like I could predict the behavior of any real-world system. Yet, when I first grasped the meaning of the Yiddish proverb, "Man plans, God laughs," I was able, for the first time, to plan complex personal and professional strategies while accepting, albeit reluctantly, the inevitability of the unexpected and the necessity to be ready to regroup, reassess, and redeploy. In this example, knowledge made me a very effective strategist, while wisdom helped me strategize with less anxiety and more calm.

As we can see, each of the previous examples has two parts. The first regards knowledge, while the second regards wisdom. It is the latter that allowed me to make better use of the former.

The Birth of the Seven Distinctions

Every significant step forward in my journey of personal and professional development has been the result of pinpointing a key distinction between two important aspects of my life or the world around me. These distinctions were gradually brought to light as I integrated newfound wisdom with previously acquired knowledge. Such distinctions were between ideas, principles, or experiences that, until then, I had misunderstood.

After carefully reviewing my new inventory of distinctions, I found that seven were at the core of my new worldview. They have allowed me to rescue myself from much inner struggle and to achieve my most challenging goals. The seven distinctions are

THE SEVENTH DISTINCTION

the following:

1. **Complication vs. Complexity:**
   The Rise of Simplicity.
2. **Understanding vs. Learning:**
   The Rise of Evolution.
3. **Management vs. Influence:**
   The Rise of Leadership.
4. **Talent vs. Personality:**
   The Rise of Competency.
5. **Ambition vs. Mission:**
   The Rise of Vision.
6. **Obligation vs. Conviction:**
   The Rise of Principle.
7. **Ego vs. Self:**
   The Rise of Consciousness.

For every distinction, we will see that neither term is intrinsically better than the other. They both hold the potential for positive and negative results. The challenge is to balance them wisely so we can make use of the third element they reveal.

The two words in each distinction might even suggest a contradiction. Yet that should cause no concern. In the words of Alfred North Whitehead, "In formal logic, a contradiction is the signal of defeat, but, in the evolution of real knowledge, it marks the first step in progress toward a victory."[2] Of course,

Introduction

by "real knowledge," Whitehead means wisdom.

Over the last twenty years, I have had the opportunity to test, adjust, and further develop these distinctions to solve real-life problems of individuals and organizations alike. As a result, the seven distinctions are at the center of my professional approach as a consultant, coach, and mentor. Also, I often deliver keynotes on the relevance of these distinctions to leaders, entrepreneurs, athletes, teachers, and other professionals.

How to Read This Book

Every chapter in this book is dedicated to one of the seven distinctions. The sequence in which they are originally presented is designed to help you explore your life in a gradually introspective fashion, from the hurdles presented by complex systems at large to the particular challenges of self-discovery. Yet the chapters can be read in any order, depending on what subjects you are more passionate about.

In general, I would suggest that people mostly interested in engineering, science, and technology, read the chapters in its original order, from one to seven. Those predominantly interested in psychology, behavior, coaching, and matters of the mind and soul, read the chapters in reverse order, from seven to one. And folks chiefly interested in business, leadership, and entrepreneurship, read the chapters in the

THE SEVENTH DISTINCTION

following sequence: three, four, five, one, two, six, and seven. Of course, these are just suggestions. Every chapter stands strongly on its own, so you can read them as you see fit.

The title of this book, *The Seventh Distinction,* points to the fact that, regardless of the order in which you read the distinctions, it is the seventh, "Ego vs. Self: The Rise of Consciousness," the one that makes all the others possible and binds them together.

Let the journey commence.

CHAPTER ONE

Complication vs. Complexity: The Rise of Simplicity

Complication A possible result of our actions.	*vs.*	**Complexity** The nature of reality regardless of our actions.

"The art of art, the glory of expression and the sunshine of the light of letters is simplicity. Nothing is better than simplicity." Walt Whitman.[3]

We live in a dynamic, challenging, sometimes hostile world. If we want to be a successful participant therein, we must compete fiercely and strive for excellence. A key question, however, is whether we can do so and still remain well-balanced.

Is it possible to compete successfully in today's world while remaining psychologically sane and physically healthy? What happens when survival, ambition, and the frenetic quest for protagonism take our inner self hostage? Up to what point can we exert ourselves without ripping our human core? The answer to this question is, to a large extent, dependent on our ability to decipher and resolve the

THE SEVENTH DISTINCTION

complexity of the world around us. That is, our ability to simplify—not avoid—our challenges, in a way that makes them easier to overcome; and our ability to simplify—not lower—our objectives, in a way that makes them easier to achieve.

In this regard, the distinction between complication and complexity is crucial for those trying to conquer simplicity as the optimal way to navigate life and fulfill their vision.

What Is Complexity?

The idea of complexity is rooted in the notions of interconnectedness and change. Since all aspects of life, including family, business, politics, religion, and everything else, are interconnected, either directly or indirectly and constantly engendering change, we can safely say that complexity is an intrinsic trait of our world.

For instance, if we took a random business and studied it, we would quickly discover that it is complex by design. We would realize that many factors determine its performance, from shareholders, managers, and employees to clients, competitors, and government regulatory agencies. Additionally, we would recognize the need to account for broader aspects of the economy and society, such as technology trends, international affairs, and demographics in order to understand fully how this business operates.

As stated earlier, we would inevitably conclude that the business is a complex entity. If we wanted to manage it successfully, we would have to observe and analyze each of its parts in detail so we can understand the whole, and vice versa.

What Is a Complication?

A complication, on the other hand, is the first sign that a complex situation has been misunderstood and dealt with inappropriately. A complication is, in fact, the very definition of a problem, and it is most often unwelcome. What is important to realize here is that, in most cases, complications are the product of our actions, not an inevitable consequence of the natural world by design. Most complications are the result of bad decisions, not of natural disasters or freaky accidents; although, the latter also happen.

Let us go back to the business example to further illustrate the nature of a complication. Let us imagine that, in an extreme case of mismanagement, we failed to identify the business's key clients, high-performing employees, and closest competitors. What would happen? Well, the result would be disastrous. We would generate major losses by making profitable clients leave; destroy morale by provoking the resignation of competent employees; and weaken the business's market position by strengthening its

THE SEVENTH DISTINCTION

competitors. This, in addition, would likely be the source of additional stress, clouding our judgement further and making us more erratic, thus worsening the situation. This is how we would take the inherent complexity of the business and turn it into a host of complications.

Complications Are Not Negative by Definition

Complications, although undesirable, are not necessarily negative when they first arise. They are the messengers that warn us about our misdoings. If we address complications in a timely manner with good disposition and judgement, they will provide us with the necessary information to reframe the situation at hand and change our course of action.

The challenge is that, in most cases, complications are actually the result of our lack of good disposition and judgement (e.g., indifference, anxiety, arrogance, etc.) to fulfill our daily responsibilities properly. So, as it would be expected, we would be unlikely to develop, all of a sudden, the good disposition and judgement we were initially lacking. This is usually the start of a vicious cycle that can bring a family, organization, or nation to its demise. Yet there is always a way out down the path of humility, self-assessment, and personal development, which we will explore in Chapter Seven.

Systems Thinking

Systems thinking is the capacity to break down complexity into its fundamental components and describe the patterns of interaction among them. This approach allows for a balanced understanding of the whole and its comprising parts, which is crucial for the solution of any problem. In summary, systems thinking is the tool we use to approach every situation and problem as a system, that is, as a collection of interconnected moving parts that must be identified, understood, and mastered.

Complex problems, in particular, tend to behave in ways that defy predictions based on common sense alone.[4] That is why it is so important to apply systems thinking in order to understand them and solve them successfully.

Leverage in Solving Complex Problems

In the same way a lever helps us move a heavy object, leverage helps us solve a complex problem. From a systemic point of view, leverage is the ability of just a few variables to produce a widespread impact within a system of many more variables. Such few variables are called leverage factors and they become visible by applying systems thinking to a complex situation. Leverage factors, if misidentified and mismanaged, tend to become the root causes of

THE SEVENTH DISTINCTION

complex problems. By the same token, correcting the unwanted behavior of leverage factors is the best way to solve, or start to solve, complex problems.

Let us proceed to identify the leverage factors in a fictitious business problem. Let us imagine we have been running a business with less-than-satisfactory sales for some time. The poor bottom line may have several causes, which are initially unknown, with different levels of impact. Yet, no matter how many causes there are, we know there must be a few that bear most of the weight. Why? Because every business is a complex entity by design and, thus, behaves like a complex system subject to the enhanced influence of a few leverage factors.

Consequently, after further scrutiny, we will undoubtedly find that the root causes of the problem lie in the distortion of a few of the organization's leverage factors. These may be the usual suspects, such as deficient leadership, an unmeritocratic corporate culture, lack of a strategic vision, slow adaptation, or absence of innovation. However, they may also lie in unexpected areas, which can only be discovered through detailed observation and analysis. In any case, the challenge will be in applying systems thinking effectively to the problem at hand. This will allow us to identify the leverage factors spawning a negative ripple effect all throughout the organization, thus undermining performance and shrinking the bottom line. This will be the beginning of the solution.

Leverage and the Rise of Simplicity

Detecting the leverage factors within a complex system is the very definition of simplicity. This allows us to determine the root causes of any problem and surgically design solutions for them. This way, we invest the least amount of effort and obtain the best possible results. Hence, we can state that the ultimate goal of systems thinking is to achieve simplicity.

However, identifying the root causes of a complex problem may be tricky. In the words of the late Jay W. Forrester, founder of System Dynamics and former professor at the MIT Sloan School of Management, "…in complex dynamic systems, causes are often far removed in both time and space from the symptom. True causes may lie far back in time and arise from an entirely different part of the system from when and where the symptoms occur."[5] That is why, when trying to solve a complex problem, we must observe the system in detail over an extended period of time. This is the only way to discover the identity, location, and influence patterns of the root causes.

Achieving actual simplicity involves conscious

THE SEVENTH DISTINCTION

observation, detailed analysis, and model building. Most importantly, though, it requires the willingness to act upon the conclusions resulting from the preceding steps. Most individuals and organizations fail to invest the necessary time and effort in observation, analysis, and model building. And, out of the few that do, most fail to commit to act based on the resulting conclusions. That is why high-performing individuals and organizations are very rare.

Complications Most Often Precede Simplicity

Since complex systems cannot be mastered before we actually immerse ourselves in them, complications are, by definition, inevitable. They will arise as part of the learning process. Therefore, complications are indeed the source of simplicity—it is by spotting and removing the former that we achieve the latter. We need the yin to get the yang. It is the nature of the world in which we live.

CHAPTER TWO

Understanding vs. Learning: The Rise of Evolution

Understanding		Learning
What happens within the mind.	*vs.*	What happens within the being.

"The tide of evolution carries everything before it, thoughts no less than bodies, and persons no less than nations." George Santayana.[6]

The words **understanding** and **learning** are usually used as direct synonyms. However, I have found that there is a big difference between them from a behavioral point of view. This difference explains the transition between knowing the path to simplicity and actually achieving simplicity.

Let us start by defining each word in detail.

Understanding

For the purposes of this book, we will characterize understanding with the very same definition we used for systems thinking in Chapter One. This is based on the premise that everything that

THE SEVENTH DISTINCTION

exists can be considered a system or part of a system. Understanding, then, is the capacity to break down reality into its fundamental components and describe the patterns of interaction among them. This approach allows for the construction of working models of real situations, thus translating complexity into simplicity.

Thanks to our capability to understand, human beings can apply categories to what we see, hear, taste, smell, and touch in the real world. We can also establish connections among such categories and arrange them into dynamic models so we can predict future events. We call the foregoing knowledge and we use it to make our everyday experiences intelligible.

As we can see, while understanding is stimulated by the tangible, outside world, it actually happens only in our minds. Similarly, knowledge, the result of understanding, is stored also only in our minds. Hence, understanding and knowledge only exist in the realm of thought.

The Conditional Structure of the Thinking Process

When we exercise our ability to think, what we are doing is connecting ideas through conditional statements. All conditional statements meet the following pattern: "IF something happens to one variable, THEN something else will happen to the same or another variable." George Boole elaborated on this premise in his book *An Investigation of the Laws of Thought*. There, Boole proposed that every person's thought process strings together the following logical operators in conditional statements:

- IF (root conditional),
- AND (dependent conditional),
- OR (independent conditional), and
- THEN (conclusive statement or resulting action).[7]

According to George Boole, human beings understand topics, situations, and problems based upon our ability to consider cause-effect relationships in the form of conditional statements. These conditional statements describe patterns that are systemic in nature, thus helping us model reality in our minds.

After many years of applying Boole's laws, I have identified two main types of conditional statements. That is, two main types of understanding, namely, Objective Understanding and Self-understanding. Let us define each in detail.

1) **Objective Understanding** is the capacity to model and predict the behavior of external variables in nature and society. This way, we can

THE SEVENTH DISTINCTION

master our surroundings and optimize the use of the resources available therein. Objective Understanding is at the core of science, technology, and business, among other fields.

2) **Self-understanding** is the capacity to model and predict human behavior by decoding our psyche and decision-making process. Self-understanding is at the core of psychology, mental health, and personal development, among other fields. By integrating Self-understanding and Objective Understanding, we can predict the impact of our actions on ourselves and our surroundings.

The following tables *(pages 22 and 23)* show examples of how our minds work when undergoing each type of understanding. The examples are set in the context of a business acquisition. As we will see, both types are different but complementary.

Example of Objective Understanding
*IF a corporation buys a competing company, **THEN** the corporation's total sales will certainly be larger immediately after the acquisition. Yet its long-term sales are uncertain because they depend on how well the new and old companies' cultures will blend.*
However, *IF a corporation buys a competing company **AND** makes investments in cultural integration, **THEN** the corporation's total sales will certainly be larger immediately after the acquisition **AND** will be likely to increase in the long term as a result of the synergies realized through cultural integration.*

Example of Self-understanding
IF *I fear criticism because it makes me feel guilty and rejected,* ***THEN*** *my objective will be to avoid mistakes.*   ***IF*** *my objective is to avoid mistakes,* ***THEN*** *I will pursue perfection in an obsessive manner.*   ***IF*** *I pursue perfection in an obsessive manner,* ***THEN*** *I will most likely experience paralysis by analysis, including its resulting anxiety, self-absorption, and lack of execution. As a result, I will most likely **get stuck** in the screening process of potential competing companies to purchase and potential cultural integration consultants to hire.*   ***IF*** *I manage to complete the acquisition and integration successfully without healing my obsessive pursuit of perfection,* ***THEN*** *I will most likely have experienced the project with much anguish that was not required for success.*

Despite having different focuses, both types of understanding are interconnected. Each type of understanding has the potential to trigger the other in ways that are unpredictable, mysterious, and fascinating. This explains phenomena like intuition, creativity, epiphanies, etc. However, as shown in the previous table, Self-understanding is the one that holds the individual responsible for his or her actions.

THE SEVENTH DISTINCTION

Learning

While understanding happens in the mind, learning happens in the entirety of a person (mind, heart, and body.) While understanding translates into new knowledge, learning translates into new behaviors. In this regard, learning can be defined as the modification of our behavior due to the desire to change some aspect of ourselves or the world around us.

The possibility for learning is created by means of an exploratory conditional statement of the form "IF I want to change this or that, THEN what should I do?"

Drawing from the examples in the previous tables, we could wonder, *"**IF** I want to increase my corporation's sales through targeted acquisitions **AND** effective cultural integration, **THEN** what company should I acquire **AND** what cultural integration consultant should I hire?"* Furthermore, we could wonder, *"**IF** I want to break free from perfectionism and its resulting anxiety, self-absorption, and lack of execution, **THEN** what should I do?"*

When such exploratory statements are triggered by a deeply rooted feeling of love, hope, pain, or fear, learning can actually take place. A heartfelt quest for giving, accomplishment, healing, or protection, respectively, is necessary to change our behavior. Without them, whatever we might have already understood will hardly translate into new behaviors.

Two Main Types of Learning

Just as I identified two main types of understanding, I also identified two main types of learning that stem from the former. The two main types of learning are **Skill Learning** and **Transformational Learning**. Let us explore each in detail.

Skill Learning, as its name implies, allows us to develop skills. It consists of behavioral changes aimed at better manipulating the resources available to us. Skill Learning builds upon Objective Understanding and is at the core of scientific, technological, and business progress.

By combining the previous example of Objective Understanding with a heartfelt quest for, say, achievement, we would experience Skill Learning. In such a case, we would develop the necessary skills to complete our business acquisition successfully. We would cultivate analytical and relational skills that would allow us to purchase the best possible company and hire the best possible consulting firm for cultural integration. This would

THE SEVENTH DISTINCTION

prove crucial in order to increase sales sustainably in the long term.

Yet we might still be under the yoke of perfectionism, feeling anxious, insecure, and fearful of the future. In such a case, we would need to experience Transformational Learning.

Transformational Learning consists of behavioral changes aimed at becoming a better person as we honestly pursue personal mastery, leadership, and peak performance. Transformational Learning builds upon Self-understanding. This type of learning does not change our essence, but it does change the nature of our connections with our inner and outer worlds. It makes us more aware, responsible, joyful, and thankful. In so doing, Transformational Learning also helps us experience Skill Learning more effectively.

By combining the previous example of Self-understanding with a heartfelt quest for, say, healing, we would experience Transformational Learning. In such a case, we would discover that, in our pursuit of perfection, there is an insecure ego crying for attention. We would also realize that our fear of criticism is rooted in a built-in sense of guilt that was probably developed during childhood. We would then conclude that we must rid ourselves of said sense of guilt and allow ourselves to make mistakes—that is the only way to experience any kind of learning. And, finally, just as we would responsibly rectify and apologize to others for our mistakes, we must also accept and forgive ourselves for them. This is the ultimate victory of anyone previously suffocated by perfectionism.

Preliminary Types of Learning

Transformational Learning requires that we face our innermost fears. In order to do so successfully, we must feel the utmost commitment to ourselves and summon the utmost courage. In such a process, we might temporarily lose perspective, sabotage ourselves, or go down the wrong road. As we battle through such pitfalls, we may undergo two preliminary phases, namely, **Flat Learning** and **Tension Learning**. Let us explore each in detail.

Flat Learning consists of cosmetic changes in behavior that have no significant impact in the results because the underlying mentality is not transformed.

If we did not achieve Self-understanding as illustrated in the previous example, we would not realize how the avoidance of guilt leads to our obsession for perfection. Hence, we would continue to be trapped in said obsession. Nonetheless, in the search for a better quality of life, we would still attempt several measures to mitigate the anxiety, self-

THE SEVENTH DISTINCTION

absorption, and lack of execution resulting from perfectionism. Such measures could include taking on a more manageable work schedule or enrolling in some type of physical exercise program. Yet, in our minds, said attempts would be aimed at getting rid of the negative consequences of perfectionism only because they stand in the way of achieving perfection. As we can see, we would be trapped in a vicious cycle.

As a result, the anxiety, self-absorption, and lack of execution are never actually overcome. This happens because our built-in sense of guilt and its resulting fear of criticism remain invisible, so the obsession remains basically unstoppable. The only way out of this maze would be to achieve Self-understanding and experience Transformational Learning.

Tension Learning consists of behavioral changes resulting from trying to modify the sought objective through self-reprograming. This strategy goes much further than Flat Learning as the conscious self-talk does have an impact. However, the self-reprogramming will never fully do the job unless the fear triggering the old objective is identified and overcome.

In other words, unless Self-understanding takes place, the underlying fear will battle the self-reprogramming, thus unleashing a war with no end. Every improvement in behavior will be the product of an internal tension and not an internal release. This will always result in the return of the old habit when exhaustion from constant self-reprogramming takes over.

If we did not achieve Self-understanding as illustrated in the previous example, we would not realize how the avoidance of guilt triggers our obsession for perfection. Nonetheless, we would be aware that our perfectionism takes a terrible toll on our health and imposes delays in execution that may prove extremely costly. Therefore, we would tell ourselves that we should no longer pursue perfection. We would tell ourselves that we should make educated decisions and deal with their consequences as they arise.

We could strengthen such self-reprogramming by elaborating on deeper ideas such as, "Perfection is not an objective concept since there is no perfect scale to measure it"; "Perfection, if feasible, would mean the end of all progress and evolution for perfection cannot be improved"; etc.

However, if we did not get rid of our built-in sense of guilt and its resulting fear of criticism, we would always feel tempted to go back to perfectionism. This would cause the need for endless

THE SEVENTH DISTINCTION

additional self-reprogramming, which could easily degenerate into a new obsession. The only way to solve this riddle would be to achieve Self-understanding and experience Transformational Learning.

Integrating Understanding and Learning into Evolution

As established earlier in this chapter, human progress is the result of Objective Understanding and Skill Learning. This is how humankind first produced and replicated fire and, millennia later, put a man on the moon. It is progress that explains the conception of the assembly line, the achievement of mass production, and the optimization of economies of scale. Objective Understanding allows us to comprehend our environment and Skill Learning allows us to master said environment. Yet this is no guarantee for a future worth living.

It is also thanks to progress that the world has been under siege time and time again. Scientific progress produced the nuclear bomb and the threat of total nuclear annihilation. Industrial progress stands behind the threat of irreversible climate and ecological damage. Military progress in industrialized nations has created secondary markets for weapons used in bloody, never-ending wars in Africa, the Middle East, and Latin America.

Progress has no moral compass—its only purpose is to make processes and devices more powerful without regard to ultimate consequences. Progress is as equally capable to end world hunger as it is to cause human extinction. As established before, progress allows us to master the environment, but it does not help us to master ourselves. This could be a recipe for disaster.

Evolution, on the other hand, is completely different from progress. Furthermore, human evolution is different from the evolution of all other living species. Charles Darwin defined evolution as the survival of the fittest within and across species. In the case of humankind, however, we have gone way beyond that premise. We strive to give the circumstantially weaker a fighting chance. This way we ensure the largest possible number of people have the opportunity to fulfill their deepest aspirations. This is because, in addition to survival, we humans also strive for happiness and transcendence, individually and collectively.

Human evolution is achieved through Self-understanding and Transformational Learning as defined earlier. This book is meant to help us evolve in the human sense.

CHAPTER THREE

Management vs. Influence: The Rise of Leadership

Management		**Influence**
Administration, analysis, optimization, allocation, structure.	*vs.*	Inspiration, commitment, empowerment, trust, enthusiasm.

"The foundation of effective leadership is thinking through the organization's mission, defining it, and establishing it, clearly and visibly. The leader sets the goals, sets the priorities, and sets and maintains the standards." Peter Drucker.[8]

Management and influence are two different skill sets that are hardly present within the same individual. In the very few cases that they are, it is because the individual has undergone a profound process of personal and professional growth. This growth, when put to the task with other people, translates into the kind of leadership that makes collective performance better.

In order to integrate management and influence, we must have a high level of technical knowledge

THE SEVENTH DISTINCTION

and a heartfelt commitment to those who accompany us. When we succeed at achieving the foregoing, our leadership flows as a natural phenomenon. This is because most people, in their pursuit of success, choose to follow those who know how to overcome the challenges at hand, both technical and relational.

A Little History: It Was Not Always About Management vs. Influence

Management vs. Influence was not initially the key distinction in the leadership debate. The distinction that first caught the attention of the corporate world was that between management and leadership. This distinction was first pointed out by Harvard Business School Professor Abraham Zaleznik in his 1977 article "Managers and Leaders: Are They Different?" In this article, Professor Zaleznik claimed that management and leadership are different in nature and seldom developed by the same individual.[9] According to this notion, people who become good managers have grown in a direction that hampers the development of their own leadership skills. Likewise, people who become good leaders have grown in a direction that hampers the development of their own management skills. This became the mainstream paradigm.

Following this viewpoint, leadership is usually defined as the ability to work with the human side of organizations in order to generate the necessary motivation and commitment to improve performance. Management, in turn, is usually defined as the ability to handle the technical side of organizations, which requires knowledge about business, operations, and the like.

I, years ago, wrote articles and delivered keynotes based on the foregoing paradigm. Nevertheless, after more than a decade of consulting and research work, I arrived at a different conclusion. I found that **really good leaders**—those who support others in the pursuit and achievement of shared goals—are also **good managers**. The reason is simple. In order to lead an organization successfully, leaders must understand the work their teams are doing, and, equally important, they must be able to do said work themselves when necessary. This finding contradicts the mainstream paradigm.

Bound by the mainstream paradigm, many organizations have justified their so-called leaders' lack of management skills as an acceptable tradeoff for their relational and inspirational skills. This overexerts the rest of the organization and decreases its motivation, commitment, and performance.

THE SEVENTH DISTINCTION

A New Paradigm: Effective Leaders Are Also Good Managers

I define management and leadership as follows. Management, on the one hand, is the ability to achieve the objectives in sight by efficiently using the available resources. For this, the manager must envision and implement a pertinent strategy, design and implement the appropriate processes, and design and assemble the necessary structure. Leadership, on the other hand, is a personality profile that combines the skill set of management with the ability to influence others in ways that strengthen the operation. For this, the leader must, in addition to managing the operation, help collaborators realize higher levels of enthusiasm and commitment in the pursuit of the objective in sight. This will allow the organization to learn all that is necessary to succeed.

The preceding definitions of management and leadership introduce a radical change to the mainstream paradigm. Leadership is actually the result of the masterful integration of management and influence. This stands as a new and different approach from the traditional distinction between management and leadership as independent skill sets.

According to what I have consistently observed in the organizational realm, the mainstream leadership paradigm has a fundamental flaw. It errs in that it remains unknowingly caught up in the confusion between leadership and influence. Leadership and influence are significantly different since the former includes the latter, but the latter alone is by no means the former.

It is one thing to influence a group of people with our words and actions. It is another to lead them to the accomplishment of a specific goal by overcoming together the customary challenges of every enterprise worth pursuing.

Influence does not require that the influencer know about the job the influenced is doing. A carpenter can influence a blacksmith, a medical doctor can influence an athlete, and a priest can influence a lawyer. In fact, even if separated by thousands of miles in space and centuries in time, one person can still influence another through storytelling and historical evidence. In none of those cases, though, has leadership taken place.

Leadership is much more. In order for leadership to take place, influence has to come with the forging of a close working relationship between the leader and the followers. A relationship that is strongly bound by the practical considerations of the task at hand. This helps the people being led to develop a higher level of trust. A leader must be available not only to inspire but also to offer practical mentorship

THE SEVENTH DISTINCTION

when followers become unable to resolve the technical challenges facing them. That means a leader has to be an influencer and a manager.

The New Paradigm Is Not So New

What is curious is that this "new" paradigm is not so new. The father of modern management theory, Peter Drucker, had already established it in some form in many of his pioneering books.

In fact, in his 1954 book *The Practice of Management*, Drucker postulated the three-dimensional nature of organizational leadership, which combines management and influence in order to achieve sustainable success. Drucker began the first chapter by saying, "The manager is the dynamic life-giving element in every business. Without his leadership the 'resources of production' remain resources and never become production."[10] He then continued, "Management is also a distinct and a leading group in industrial society."[11]

Later, in his 1973 book *Management: Tasks, Responsibilities, Practices*, Drucker stated, "The fact is that in modern society there is no other leadership group but managers. If the managers of our major institutions, and especially of business, do not take responsibility for the common good, no one else can or will."[12]

The Rise of Leadership

Other more contemporary authors have also pointed to the paradigm established in this chapter. For instance, Jack Welch, considered one of the world's top leadership gurus, has written and spoken about his leadership principles in a language that is deeply motivational and also strongly managerial.

More specifically, in his bestselling book *Jack: Straight from the Gut*, Welch describes his own leadership experience as GE's former CEO. He does so by combining principles of influence and management in a dynamic continuum that seems indivisible. In this book, Welch highlighted the importance of helping employees conquer self-confidence and making sure top performers learn from their mistakes. This is definitely a reference to the importance of positive influence. Yet he also emphasized how critical it was for GE to move from low-margin, low-growth industries to high-margin, high-growth ones in order to achieve sustained growth. This is definitely a reference to the importance of good management. Furthermore, Welch made a special reference to how important it was for GE to move into businesses with competitive advantages instead of comparative advantages, in order to reduce volatility.[13] This is another clear allusion to the significance of good management.

For a leader to understand the relevance of Welch's full exposition, he or she must be familiar

THE SEVENTH DISTINCTION

with Michael Porter's Five Forces, the difference between competitive and comparative advantages, and many other management and economic models. A so-called leader who is fixated in matters of influence, motivation, etc., with no handle on management, would find Welch's exposition quite discouraging.

In my opinion, without explicitly stating so, Welch believes that in order to be a good leader, the individual also has to be a good manager. Otherwise, Welch would not make references to sound management principles when talking about leadership.

Good Leaders Are Also Good Managers: It Is a Matter of Responsibility

Mainstream authors believe that good leaders can compensate for their lack of management skills by surrounding themselves with good managers. This premise, however, is fundamentally misaligned with my findings. In my experience, successful leaders must be able to support or reject, with good judgment, the advice given by the other managers. The only way for leaders to do so is by having well developed management skills themselves.

Put differently, a so-called good leader who blindly and naïvely supports the advice of so-called good managers is playing the lottery with the fate of the organization. While some people may dare call that trust and empowerment, I call it negligence and lack of responsibility. Trust is not faith, and empowerment is not delegating all judgement to others. Trust is believing in another individual's competency after sufficient proof has been provided to that end. Empowerment, in turn, is delegating critical tasks to other people with minimum supervision but not a total lack thereof. This is world-class leadership because it has a management backbone. This is how we move an organization forward.

People in leadership positions who lack management skills are often threatened by those who do have them. Sometimes, these undeserving leaders will end up losing their positions, thus rendering themselves useless or fundamentally transforming their roles. Others will protect their undeserved leadership position at all cost by resorting to the kind of political maneuvering and dirty play that can make a workplace unbearable to most.

Let us not mistake this critique to the mainstream approach to leadership for a suggestion that leaders should do all the micromanagement. That is definitely not the job of effective leaders. What I mean is that leaders must have the professional judgment and responsible involvement in order to monitor, make informed decisions, and YES, manage when necessary. Even if the managers who report to the leader are endowed with super human management skills, the leader must be able to form a detailed opinion about what is being done. Otherwise, he or she would not be adding value. It is very simple: No one can lead an operation whose management completely escapes them.

Managers Can Provide Purpose

Many authors claim that managers are focused on execution, control, and continuance, whereas leaders provide purpose and introduce constructive challenges. Such a paradigm, however, contradicts what I have witnessed firsthand as a speaker, coach, and consultant. Most managers do provide purpose, and, given the right circumstances, they can also introduce constructive challenges.

For instance, a good manager may have a clear vision of how to improve efficiency. Such a vision could be so innovative as to transform the core structure of a whole industry. However, if such a forward-looking manager lacks the necessary influence skills to bring everyone on board, then he or she will fail to become a leader. Therefore, in this case, it is not the lack of purpose, as it is traditionally argued, but the inability to share it persuasively with others that hinders leadership.

If managers, in general, want to fulfill their purpose and realize their vision, they must develop the necessary influence skills to share them effectively with others. By doing this, they can become leaders within the organization in which they are already good managers.

The Challenge: Integrating Management and Influence

Based on what has been presented so far, the main challenge when developing leadership is to develop both management and influence in a balanced way. Some people tend to lean too much toward the straightforward applicability of management techniques in detriment to the complex relational competencies demanded by influence. However, other people tend to rely too much on the powerful impact, and sometimes dazzling flavor, of influence in detriment to the indispensable management techniques that make the operation feasible. Aiming for both is what makes a true leader.

CHAPTER FOUR

Talent vs. Personality: The Rise of Competency

Talent		Personality
What you can do.	vs.	What you have become or have chosen to be.

"We should take care not to make the intellect our god; it has, of course, powerful muscles, but no personality." Albert Einstein.[14]

In the 1970s, there was a growing realization that the number-one factor behind a business's performance was its people. This led to the investment of vast amounts of resources to harness and develop human potential. One of the most immediate results was the evolution from the traditional **human resources** departments to the more up-to-date **human talent management** departments. Such progression revealed an evolution in the mentality about the role of people in the creation of value. From this transformational current also came the term "competency" and the broader management approach known as "competency-based management."

THE SEVENTH DISTINCTION

Yet, in the midst of so much change in the field of people management, a crucial factor has gone widely overlooked. This factor is personality. Most approaches emphasize, and almost worship, talent as the ultimate tool for achieving sustainable high performance. However, I have found that it is personality that ultimately produces and sustains high performance. If talent is a power tool, personality is the electricity that powers it.

Talent, Personality and the Rise of Competency

Talent is the capability to perform a task by executing specific actions or displaying specific behaviors. Talents can be inborn or developed by training. Similarly, talents can be cognitive, artistic, physical, behavioral, or some combination thereof. Being a persuasive communicator, an insightful poet, an innovative scientist, or a fast swimmer is partly the result of having a specific talent or set of talents. Talents are also called skills, abilities, or aptitudes depending on the author. Some scholars have also drawn differences among the latter three in order to fine-tune the blueprint of human capabilities. However, for the sake of simplicity, we will assume they are all the same.

Personality, on the other hand, is a far more complex component of the human condition. It is so complex that there are almost as many personality models as there are authors who have theories on the subject. In the midst of this mixture, I have attempted to integrate the similarities among the major personality models into a simple model that will serve us for the rest of this book. As you will see, most of the components of this model are further explored in the following chapters. Yet their mere mention here is enough to convey the inherent complexity of personality.

According to this simple model, an individual's personality is made up of the following essential components:

1) The Self (The real I);
2) The Ego (The apparent self);
3) Consciousness (The individual's level of awareness of, and mastery over, the self, the ego, and the rest of the components of this model);
4) Motivation (Primal emotion for self-realization);
5) Fear (Primal emotions for survival);
6) Anger (Primal emotion for self-vindication);
7) Biological instincts (Search for pleasure and comfort, and avoidance of pain and suffering; influencers of motivation, fear, and anger);
8) The unconscious (Unknown potential for the expansion of consciousness); and
9) Intuition (Connection between the unconscious and consciousness, thus helping reveal more about the self and the outside world).

THE SEVENTH DISTINCTION

As can be seen, it is significantly more challenging to get a grip on personality than to get a grip on talent. The impact of personality on our behavior is far greater than that of talent. So much so, in fact, that personality can either enhance or override any talent at any time. Personality is, in practical terms, the repository of our sense of identity and purpose, so talent is always subjected to personality.

The Rise of Competency

The distinction between talent and personality also provides the groundwork for the definition of **competency**. Many definitions have been given for this term over time, many of which can be equated back to talent, ability, and aptitude. However, I have come to realize that a competency is much more than that. A competency encompasses the behavioral portfolio that results from the combination of certain talents and certain personality traits. Competencies, which make us competent and competitive at what we do, result from channeling our talents through the amplifying and targeting effects of our personality. Talents alone lack the launching platform of personality and, therefore, can remain unused, misused, or unimproved for years.

A highly developed competency can be the result of combining a small, apparently irrelevant talent with a conscious, mature, and driven personality. Likewise, a poorly developed competency can be the result of combining a wide portfolio of flashy talents with a rambling, immature, and insecure personality.

The Role of Competencies in Human Organizations

Modern organizations invest a considerable amount of resources in the development of competency-based management models. I have worked on numerous projects of this nature as a management consultant, leadership trainer, and executive coach. In most of those instances, I realized that my clients had an initial one-sided stand in favor of talent with little or no regard for personality. My first question to them was always, "Why so much focus on the desired 'doing' and so little focus on the 'doer?'" After asking this question too many times, I came to the conclusion that, for most people, by means of developing talents, the individual is also developed. Yet my observations indicate something different.

I have found that by developing talents alone, whatever the individual is will be amplified, not necessarily improved. That is, the individual's ego will be strengthened. So, if the individual does not have additional tools to explore and manage his or her ego, the further development of talents may create unforeseen negative results.

Talents alone allow us to discover what we can do today and in the future. Personality, on the other hand, allows us to discover who we are today and who we want to become in the future. We need a sense of identity and purpose in order to exploit our potential in full. This is how we master ourselves, lead others to master themselves, and achieve peak performance.

The following table presents a selection of commonly designated talents. On the next page, another table presents the Psychological Types designated by Carl Gustav Jung, a well-known personality-type model. By asking how each personality type would use and develop each talent, we can immediately see the defining impact of personality on the use of talents.

Selection of Talents
- Logical reasoning
- Symbolic thinking
- Abstract thinking
- Persuasion
- Empathy
- Physical athleticism
- Artistic expression

Jung's Psychological Types[15]
-**Extraverted Sensation:** Pursues the intense experience of physical activities and objects with no special attention to inner psycho-logical processes. Becomes utterly practical in the quest for pleasure and experiences in general. -**Introverted Sensation:** Pursues depth and meaning through the over-scrutinizing and resulting alterations of perceptions. Becomes wrapped in internal sensations and ignores or dismisses the objective information available in the outside world. -**Extraverted Intuition:** Strives to understand the complexity inherent in the outside world by paying great attention to details and patterns that may be invisible to most others. -**Introverted Intuition:** Strives to understand the complexity inherent in the self and inner psychological processes. Becomes immersed in a constant drawing of parallelisms between their personal experiences and universal laws or premises. -**Extraverted Thinking:** Pursues the conquest of objective knowledge, based upon proven evidence, which can be applied to achieve practical goals. -**Introverted Thinking:** Pursues the absolute understanding of ideas, principles, premises, and notions in the pursuit of infallibility of thought with no practical applicability in the horizon. -**Extraverted Feeling:** Pursues the harmonization of inner feelings and social standards, sometimes becoming trendy and style-oriented, thus making their feelings seem fake. -**Introverted Feeling:** Pursues the intense experience of the self and inner processes with sometimes a blatant disregard for others and the objective reality of the outside world. Dictates his or her actions by the subjective conclusions of the inner world.

THE SEVENTH DISTINCTION

As an example, let us select one talent—**logical reasoning**—and take it through two of Jung's Psychological Types—**Extraverted Sensation** and **Introverted Thinking**. This will help us see how each personality type translates the same talent into a different competency. Additionally, we will see how an individual's specific level of maturity impacts performance significantly within the same competency. Let us begin.

We could argue that an individual with the **Extraverted Sensation** Type would use the talent of **logical reasoning** to figure out the most effective way to derive the most joy from his or her relationships. This would translate into a competency of relationship management, which, depending on the individual's level of maturity, would render significantly different levels of performance. A mature individual would establish functional relationships of mutual benefit. A maturing individual would seek personal benefit from all relationships while also learning to acknowledge other people's interests. Finally, an immature individual would compulsively see others as objects of personal benefit, joy, or pleasure.

Similarly, we could argue that an individual with the **Introverted Thinking** Type could use the talent of **logical reasoning** to develop working models about the world and everything it contains. This

The Rise of Competency

could translate into many different competencies, such as scenario analysis, strategic planning, psychological profiling, and more. Yet, as always, the individual's level of maturity would significantly influence the resulting performance. A mature individual would develop models and apply them as useful references without becoming crippled by them. A maturing individual would struggle to accept real-life evidence that contradicted his or her models. Finally, an immature individual would reject real-life evidence and attempt to impose his or her models on others.

As we can see, if we focus on talent while ignoring or lightly brushing over personality, we are looking only at half of the picture. In fact, we are ignoring the half that defines purpose and actual investment of effort and time. My rule of thumb is that "much" personality and "little" talent can go further than "little" personality and "much" talent. Therefore, in order to develop a competency to improve performance, the individual must undergo both Skill Learning and Transformational Learning as defined in Chapter Two. This is how we improve both talent and personality.

CHAPTER FIVE

Ambition vs. Mission: The Rise of Vision

Ambition	vs.	**Mission**
Personal quest.		Collective quest.

"Your vision will become clear only when you can look into your own heart. Who looks outside, dreams; who looks inside, awakens." Carl Jung.

An **ambition** is quite different from a **mission**. Nevertheless, they are often mistaken for one another when describing someone's drive for achievement, success, and transcendence. An ambition is the desire to achieve something for the sake of personal benefit, usually disregarding its potential consequences on others. A mission, however, is the desire to achieve something for the sake of collective benefit, usually including the self.

However, despite this fundamental difference, all ambitions and missions are triggered by early experiences of non-approval, inadequacy, abuse, or rejection. The individual, driven by said experiences, embarks on a quest for personal vindication in order to restore his or her sense of self-worth. This is only

THE SEVENTH DISTINCTION

natural for we all deserve respect from others and ourselves. Yet the quest for such a vindication takes significantly different paths depending on whether it happens through the ego or through a working partnership between the ego and the self.

Ambitions

When we pursue vindications only through our egos, we start to believe erroneously that all we need is social validation. Since others are not obligated to validate us, we gradually start to resent those who do not. In so doing, we may end up attacking, rejecting, or ignoring the very people whose approval we were seeking. Finally, we may start to resent ourselves for not being able to get everyone to validate us. This is the path of ambition—unable to achieve self-validation; always full of frustration regardless of success.

An etymological reference to the word ambition may shed additional light on its underlying meaning. The word ambition comes from the Latin word *ambitionem*, meaning "'a going around,' especially to solicit votes, hence 'a striving for favor, courting, flattery; a desire for honor; thirst for popularity.'"[16] This word was first used to describe the workings of politicians in their quest for popular support. This reveals how egotistical an ambition can become and how much damage it can do to an individual's moral compass if he or she is not careful.

Yet ambitions are neither bad nor evil by definition. If we are able to reduce the dose of ego in our ambitions and allow more of our inner selves to shine through, we can actually pave the way to develop a mission of collective benefit.

Ambitions Alone: The Mirage of Success

Highly ambitious people usually cause many tensions and conflicts. They tend to be egotistical, distrustful, and over-competitive. This generates work environments where people spend most of the time defending themselves from the trespasses of others or evading the consequences of having trespassed others. In these circumstances, the job usually gets done but at a high existential cost and with many inefficiencies.

However, in today's over-competitive, individualistic society, ambition has become an admired quality in people. In fact, some ambitious personalities of popular culture are almost worshiped without regard to their catastrophic personal state of affairs. They continue to be admired because, despite an otherwise questionable life, they have achieved economic success and fame—universal ambitions. This is a Damocles' Sword in Western society, in which an individual's ambition may sometimes offset

THE SEVENTH DISTINCTION

his or her very instinct of self-preservation. Similarly, ambitions may cloud an individual's sense of community.

Missions

When we pursue vindication through a working partnership between the ego and the self, our quest becomes more conscious.

Conscious people are able to acknowledge, explore, and develop their inner selves. In so doing, they are able to develop self-validation and achieve self-realization. Furthermore, conscious people are able to acknowledge their ego's pitfalls. This makes their personal quests honest, and, most importantly, correctible when necessary.

Once the self enters the equation, the ego stands in checkmate and humility starts to flow internally. This brings down our need for social validation to a functional level and allows us to validate others. This is how a mission becomes possible, as a true mission always bears thoughtful recognition of the dignity of others.

An etymological reference to the word mission may clarify its underlying meaning. The word mission comes from the Latin word *missionem*, meaning "sending abroad, dispatching,"[17] originally used to denote the Jesuits' missions to evangelize and civilize, in their view, the indigenous people of the Americas. Despite how questionable these missions of the past may be today, the notion of going beyond one's limits to do the "right thing" for others still lies at the core of this word. Of course, we know today that the "right thing" is far different from unilaterally deciding what is good for others and imposing such a decision by force. Yet everyone who embarks on a mission is trying to realize, in their own way, what they think is right for themselves and others.

John C. Maxwell's Sixth Law of Leadership, The Law of Solid Ground,[18] comes into play when we try to do the right thing for ourselves and others. It allows every team member, especially the leader, to display the kind of competency, connection, and character necessary to keep the team together and moving forward.[19] This happens because they are able to realize synergies that would otherwise be hidden under the chaos of individual ambitions.

Selfless Mission vs. Self-Including Mission: Heroism vs. Fairness

There are those in history who pursued a mission of wide collective reach, devoid of ego, and with no regard for their own survival. We look up to them for many reasons, one of them being that they lived up to the ideals of heroism and self-sacrifice that many of

THE SEVENTH DISTINCTION

us struggle with. I consider such people to be the highest expression of human greatness. Not only did they achieve extraordinary vindications during their lifetime, but they also had the courage to risk their own lives for their cause. In fact, many of them died standing up for their principles.

People like Jesus of Nazareth, Joan of Arc, Mahatma Gandhi, and Martin Luther King, Jr., just to name a few, have helped hold our social fabric together through limitless giving. Selfless missions are inspiring.

Yet selfless missions are uncommon. When the time comes, selfless missions are followed through by very few brave ones. Most people stop when the ultimate sacrifice is the price of vindication. This, in itself, is understandable, as we all want to exercise our right to live to the fullest. This is why self-including missions tend to gain more traction in all realms of life. People tend to become more engaged when they feel they will get to enjoy the desired vindications.

Based on my findings, I believe that most vindications in society, politics, and business can be achieved through self-including missions. Self-including missions have driven the actions of conscious elected officials, business people, and citizens in general, who recognize the value of solidarity and teamwork for the sustainability of our world.

The Rise of Vision

One topic that inevitably comes up when exploring mission and ambition is that of vision. Vision is the word used most frequently in organizational theory to talk about how leaders bring people together around a specific objective for the future. In this regard, when formulating a vision, most authors recommend thinking out of the box, being creative, and stretching the imagination, so the vision will not just be a continuation of the present. The vision, according to these authors, must be a challenging, yet achievable, point of reference for action.

I recognize the practical benefits of the aforementioned approach for a quick organizational exercise. Yet I consider it shortsighted and misleading in the larger scheme of organizational development. In fact, I have a whole different approach to the word vision, which is rooted in its original meaning spanning past, present, and future.

The word **vision** comes from the Latin word *visio,* meaning "seeing, view; appearance; notion, idea,"[20] which later evolved into the Anglo-French word *visonem*, meaning "something seen in the

THE SEVENTH DISTINCTION

imagination or in the supernatural."[21]

The early meanings of the word "vision" denoted what could be seen without the eyes, meaning the mind, the soul, or by means of supernatural aid. The oracles in Greek Mythology revealed these types of visions to the passing explorer, warrior, or demigod. Such revelations were not exclusively about the future. The unknown could also be hidden in the past and the present, rendering its revelation equally useful for many purposes. The key to a vision's power was in the leverage it provided to achieve a specific objective. By revisiting its old meaning, we can boost the power of this word in today's world, which is so obsessed with the future and so dismissive of the present and the past.

The focus on the future has made today's society quite compulsive, obsessive, and, honestly, flat-out absent in its own time. In fact, most people become slaves to their own ambitions as a result of being fixated on the future and surrendering to the exhaustive demands of the ego. A vision that only sees the future is just that: an ambition.

Changing the Past, Ourselves, and the Future: Turning an Ambition into a Mission

Leadership is traditionally defined with respect to changing the future. That is why having a vision for the future is usually considered one of the key aspects of leadership. What we need to realize, though, is that if we do not change our past, we cannot change our future. This might seem counterintuitive to most, and it definitely is when looked at from a mechanical perspective of time. Yet the human psyche works differently—we cannot change the facts that already happened, but we can change the imprint they left on us.

By reframing the past, we also reframe ourselves in the present. As a result, we become able to reframe the future in ways that were previously unimaginable. When we reframe our past, we become able to heal our emotional wounds, thus becoming able to imagine a healed future. This is true Transformational Learning. As a result, we achieve the personal vindications we were erratically pursuing though our ambitions. In this regard, our ego-centered ambitions lose strength. We start to see the people around us with more compassion and realize we are all more similar than we are different. When we reach such a realization, our ambitions can now become a mission aimed at creating a better future for everyone involved. This gives our endeavors better potential for long-term sustainability.

In fact, when most authors talk about creating a vision for the future, I talk about developing a

THE SEVENTH DISTINCTION

worldview spanning past, present, and future as previously explained. This is how we use the power of today to learn from the past in order to change the future.

In Osho's words, if you do not change your past, "Whatsoever you do in the future will be a continuation of the past. You can change a little—a patch here, a patch there, but the main part will remain just the same."[22] George Santayana, in a simpler way, also expressed the same notion by writing, "Those who cannot remember the past are condemned to repeat it."[23]

Ambition and Mission in Today's Organizations

Human organizations need people who have a shared worldview. This is the only way they can transform their personal ambitions into a shared mission. Otherwise, their individual objectives will most likely run wildly out of sync, thus bringing to life Abraham Lincoln's famous quote, "A house divided against itself cannot stand."[24]

When a mission is shared among different people, they are unlikely to pursue mutually threatening objectives. Despite giving themselves room for individual pursuits, the mission they share underlies their choices, thus providing for a cohesive group dynamic.

Missions are not epic statements that make people daydream of a better world as much as they are statements that bring people together to do actual work. Organizations that embrace this philosophy relieve internal tensions through effective communication and resolve internal conflicts through negotiation. As a result, the people involved are willing to improve themselves, become better teammates, and elevate their performance in order to achieve the organization's objectives.

CHAPTER SIX

Obligation vs. Conviction: The Rise of Principle

Obligation		**Conviction**
What I do based on other people's expectations to gain approval.	vs.	What I do based on my own expectations regardless of those of other people.

"Act as if the maxim of thy action were to become by thy will a universal law of nature." Immanuel Kant.[25]

Given our social nature, we all have an intrinsic need to be accepted and appreciated by other people. Meanwhile, as we become defined individuals, we develop personal interests that we must fulfill in order to achieve self-realization. Hence, we are both a social and an individualistic species. This dual nature gives rise to the dilemma between obligations and convictions.

Put simply, whenever people are pursuing an objective mainly to get someone else's approval, they are doing it as an obligation to that person. However, whenever people are pursuing an objective regardless of someone else's approval, they are doing it out of a

THE SEVENTH DISTINCTION

personal conviction. As in all the other distinctions presented in this book, obligations and convictions are neither intrinsically good nor bad. They both hold the potential for improving and harming ourselves and the people around us.

Obligations remind us that we are not alone in the world, but they can also make us slaves to those around us. In turn, convictions let us know what we need and want to be happy, but they can also make us forget about the people around us.

Obligations benefit us when they facilitate our insertion into the social fabric that binds us all together. However, they turn into problems when fear of rejection takes over our lives. In turn, convictions benefit us when they help us make decisions aimed at our self-realization. However, they turn into problems when they are dismissive of others and their well-being.

Distinguishing between Obligations and Convictions When They Swap Suits

Obligations can sometimes be cleverly disguised as convictions in two cases. The first case is when our fear of rejection leads us to pursue total supremacy (e.g. power, popularity, glory, etc.) to ensure social approval. The second case is when our fear of rejection leads us to reject society as a defense mechanism by ignoring it, condemning it through moralistic judgment, or scandalizing it through loud extravagance.

In both cases, the individual acts out of obligation—not conviction—since his or her actions are fueled by the imperative need to attract people's attention. In fact, in both cases, the individual's first choice (i.e. conviction) would have been to get the desired approval earlier by just being him or herself without so much extra work.

In the two cases previously described, the individual's self-talk is something like, "I am just being true to myself" or "I just need my own approval." This is because the ego, when it becomes hyper-developed, appears to be the main source of demands in its own right. In such cases, though, the ego is still only responding to the demands perceived from society. When the ego reaches this level of power over the individual, it makes any process of personal growth very difficult to begin. Hardship and conflict are the story of these individuals, even when the demands of the ego are met.

A person's convictions, in turn, can be mistaken for obligations by outsiders—especially when said convictions motivate the amount and intensity of work that most people are unwilling to put into anything.

THE SEVENTH DISTINCTION

Integrating Obligations and Convictions into Principles

As a social species with self-interested individuals, we cannot dismiss either obligations or convictions. By dismissing obligations, we would become a menace to the human race. Similarly, by dismissing convictions, we would become slaves to social constructs. We must strike a balance between the two. Empathy is the key to achieve such balance.

As people willfully acknowledge the rights of others, they start to experience some obligations with the enthusiasm and determination of convictions. Similarly, they start to assess the feasibility of their own convictions in terms of their impact on others. Then, and only then, we can start to develop principles as truly actionable pieces of our personality.

A principle is a personal value that reaffirms one's right to achieve self-realization and the rights of all others to achieve theirs. Principles translate into peaceful, constructive, and sustainable coexistence among people.

The ability to integrate obligations and convictions into principles reveals the highest level of personal mastery. Furthermore, the ability to show others how to do the same reveals the highest level of leadership. And, in so doing, we can only improve our individual and collective performance.

The foregoing has led me to the conclusion that principles should not be imposed; they should be developed. When they are imposed, principles become obligations. As a result, they are more likely to be rejected than to be embraced. Laws and rules in a democracy are necessary to establish a social contract that highlights the need for respectful coexistence. However, we must find ways to develop principles from within, especially during childhood and adolescence. Family and education, not laws, are the source of principles.

Telling Convictions and Obligations Apart from Principles When They Swap Suits

On the one hand, moralistic, religious, and conservative people tend to build their lives upon obligations. On the other hand, libertarians and liberals tend to build their lives upon convictions. Both types of people, especially when they are extremists, present their personal preferences as universal principles that benefit all.

Interestingly, both extreme conservatives and extreme liberals compensate for their public tendencies by consenting to the opposite in their private lives. Extreme conservatives tend to indulge

THE SEVENTH DISTINCTION

personal convictions behind people's backs; and extreme liberals tend to feel obligated to their fellow liberals to defend their convictions. This introduces a fundamental challenge for the people of principle since, unfortunately, they tend to seem conservative to liberals and liberal to conservatives. This is because, from each extreme, the wise, balanced center is usually perceived as the opposite extreme.

Accountability vs. Responsibility

The English dictionary offers very similar definitions for these two words—so similar, indeed, that they are considered direct synonyms. However, from a behavioral point of view, accountability and responsibility are two very different prescriptions to deal with the consequences of our actions. This distinction makes a world of a difference in assessing someone's character and maturity.

Western civilization tends to condemn failure and reward success, outcast the loser and uplift the victor. In this context, there is no problem being accountable and responsible for success. Yet it will require much effort to assign accountability and responsibility for failure to a specific person or group thereof. Therefore, it will be much more valuable to define accountability and responsibility in the context of errors, mistakes, and misdoings as it is in dealing therewith that most people struggle.

Accountability is an individual's willingness to render truthful account about why and how an action was taken. This gives the people affected more elements with which to offer a more just verdict. Responsibility, in turn, is an individual's willingness to embrace and learn from the consequences of any given action. This will help the individual respond more effectively to the same challenge in the future.

Accountability is driven by the sense of social obligation to offer a valid explanation of our actions to those who were affected by them. However, responsibility is driven by the sense of personal conviction to achieve whatever objective we are pursuing.

Accountable people are not necessarily responsible as they do not necessarily embrace and learn from the consequences of their actions. Likewise, responsible people are not necessarily accountable as they do not necessarily give a truthful account of why and how an action was taken.

The question is what kind of person would learn from his or her actions and also give a truthful account thereof. Such an individual would be one of principle, acting with what I call **accountable responsibility**. Said individual would act based on a wise balance between his or her desire to succeed and the impact thereof on others.

CHAPTER SEVEN

Ego vs. Self:
The Rise of Consciousness

Ego		Self
How I want other people to see me.	vs.	The truth behind the ego.

"The truth shall set you free."
Jesus of Nazareth.

When we start to question our self-concept, choices, and reality, it is because we have come face to face with the dilemma between our ego and our inner self. We start to realize there is a difference between who we think we are and who we really are. We also start to realize there is a difference between our worldview and the real world. Such realizations may stem from a variety of reasons, such as constant confrontations with other people, repeated failures, or a grave illness. Also, the death of a loved one, a great book, or an impactful conversation may trigger that realization.

The key point, however, is that once the dilemma between our ego and our inner self arises, it never fades away unless we formally address it. We may try to hide it from others, but we will never be

THE SEVENTH DISTINCTION

able to hide it from ourselves.

It is when we choose to address this dilemma that we begin a truthful quest for identity and purpose. Addressing this dilemma has accounted for the first step in the process of personal growth of every person I have known to walk such a path. Personal mastery is nothing more than the progressive resolution of this dilemma as it is triggered by each situation and person we encounter in life.

People who have achieved high levels of personal mastery, leadership, and performance have experienced the dilemma between the ego and the self with particular intensity. That is why they feel the imperious need to address it. As they embark on such an enterprise, they start to experience personal transformations that ultimately become inspirational to others.

As we address the dilemma between our ego and our inner self, we must beware of charlatans who provide hollow solutions to this most important of concerns. Since this dilemma accounts for the core tension inside every human being, people in general are prone to fall prey to false prophets, self-titled experts, and wishy-washy therapists. The resolution of this dilemma requires commitment, courage, and a true disposition to explore unchartered territories within ourselves.

The Ego and the Self Revealed through the Help of Others

If we want to resolve the dilemma between the ego and the self, we need to develop an unequivocal sense of hope, as it is an arduous process. At the same time, we need to develop a sense of humor, as this process may sometimes seem like a cosmic joke in which we are the punch line. That being said, the best way to start tackling this dilemma is by defining both of its terms in detail.

In order to define the ego and the self properly, we must address the existence of those who surround us. Our human nature incorporates our design as a social species. No individual can fully be without those around him or her, and no group of people can fully be without every single one of its members. Therefore, in order to define the ego and the self, we must also define the Other—those who trigger the questions about the ego and the self.

Let us define, then, the ego, the self, and the other.

The Ego

The ego is the apparent self that we show to

THE SEVENTH DISTINCTION

others. It starts to develop as soon as we are born, maybe even earlier in our mother's womb. Since its purpose is to help us adapt to the world around us, we are programmed to engineer our egos on the basis of other people's expectations. First our parents, then everyone else, are the blueprints for our egos. Having this introduction to human life seems to be of the utmost importance for the continuation of civilization. Without social standards and our egos to help us adapt to them, every one of us would have to discover the world from scratch on our own—not a very efficient process. Paradoxically, that seems to be our job as adults anyway—only the world we have to discover from scratch is our inner world.

Our ego, which is at the core of our worldview, also comprises the only psychological mechanism that we can use to envision our goals and devise the necessary action plans to achieve them. Without the ego, there could be no approximation to reality. We need the ego to have paradigms, opinions, and points of views in order to make decisions. Without the ego, our brains would shut down, our bodies would drop, and we would fuse with the whole thus becoming something other than human. Our egos make us human.

The ego, as we can see, is neither good nor bad. It plays a crucial role in our lives, including our social adaptation and the attainment of our achievements. Nevertheless, it can also detach us from reality when its approximations thereto become dismissive of others' viewpoints. Furthermore, our ego can also detach us from reality when it starts to reject irrefutable evidence against its own views. It is up to each individual to keep his or her ego flexible and not let it smother his or her inner self. This is the path to personal mastery.

The Self

The self is that inner voice that tells us that we are something other than our egos. The self is a sense of individual awareness that allows us to see ourselves beyond other people's expectations. The self, once you start to define it, sounds similar to the soul, the essence, the source, and notions of that sort. The self is, in a way, an unfathomable concept, which is why we all need to build our egos first in order to have a starting point to approach it. Having our inner self manage and steer our ego is where personal mastery lies.

The self and the ego could be considered the two basic subatomic particles of human nature. They are both necessary for a healthy development of our human condition. Yet, despite this complementarity between the two, one premise is clear: the self should always supersede the ego. Put another way, the ego should be at the service of the self, not the other way

THE SEVENTH DISTINCTION

around. Let us explore this point further.

The ego is partly fueled by the fear of rejection whereas the self is partly fueled by the courage of vindication. Therefore, when fear takes over, so does the ego, and when courage takes over, so does the self. These are completely different paths.

When fear supersedes courage, the latter turns into anger, then resentment, and finally hatred. However, when courage supersedes fear, the latter turns into prudence, one of our most useful virtues and sources of wisdom. In the words of Albert Einstein, "The true measure of a man is the degree to which he has managed to subjugate his ego."

The Other and the Rise of Consciousness

The other is the people around us—those who, by interacting with us, show us our deepest truth and the effort we make to conceal it. The people around us are the mirrors that reflect what no other mirror can: the dilemma between our ego and our inner self.

When we wake up in the morning and go to the bathroom to brush our teeth, the mirror in front of us reflects our physical image. That reflection triggers multiple private conversations as we prepare ourselves to go out and project the best possible image. Then we take a shower, get dressed, and go out to the real world hoping we will follow the script we just prepared. Once out there, we face the hall of mirrors, only these mirrors do not trigger private conversations, they trigger real conversations. The hall of mirrors is made up of all the people we encounter in real life. They talk back to us or ignore us in unpredictable ways, undoing the private conversations we had in the morning.

Whether we feel calm or restless, happy or sad, enlightened or confused, our interactions with other people will evoke our inner truth. Maybe we can hide it from them, but we can never hide it from ourselves. When we finally acknowledge and embrace our inner truth, as it is revealed to us through our interactions with others, we finally become conscious.

Consciousness, in short, is the acknowledgement and development of our inner self as we learn to manage our ego. This allows for the vindication of the self in ways that are socially constructive.

By becoming conscious, as defined herein, we can successfully address and balance the other distinctions presented in this book.

The Indivisibility of Consciousness and Love

When we first experience the dilemma between the ego and the self, it is like a wakeup call. We start

THE SEVENTH DISTINCTION

wondering why we think what we think, why we feel what we feel, and why we do what we do. However, that does not mean we actually wake up and get up. We could very easily go back to sleep or remain drowsing in bed, thus leaving the questions unanswered. So, where does the ultimate motivation to get up and walk come from? I have repeatedly confirmed that the ultimate motivation is provided by someone else.

It is our love for someone else that ignites the questions and the search for the answers. In so doing, we might be confused, beaten down, or forced to close our eyes by the circumstances. Yet, as long as we continue to love that one person (or persons), we will never fall asleep again. This inexorably links love—in all its forms—with consciousness.

Egotism, Humility, and Modesty

Having already defined the ego, the self, and the other, we can address the three basic human attributes, namely, humility, egotism, and modesty. These are three behavioral pathways that arise from the way we choose to resolve the dilemma between the ego and the self in our relationships with others. Consciousness, as previously defined, will be the cornerstone of the exploration that follows.

Before getting started, let us establish that we

will not go by the definitions in the English dictionary, as they do not carry enough psychological meaning to explore human behavior.*

Therefore, for the purposes of this book, we will explore a set of definitions I have developed in the areas of personal mastery, leadership development, and performance maximization. I have found these definitions to be extremely powerful when helping myself and my clients solve complex personal and professional problems. Let us begin.

Egotism

Egotism is, as the word implies, the discipline (ism) of the ego. It is the practice of relating to others almost exclusively through our egos, thus concealing our true selves as much as possible. It is the discipline or habit of showing ourselves conveniently modified on the basis of what we believe other people's expectations are. Egotism is always unconscious in the beginning. It is rooted in what we unconsciously learned from our own relationships during childhood and adolescence. When our

---

* According to the dictionary, *humility* is synonymous with *modesty*, while *egotism* is related to *selfishness*. By the same token, humility and modesty are usually seen as positive traits, while egotism and selfishness are not. We will not go by these definitions. They are perfectly suitable for colloquial and literary use; yet they do not carry enough psychological content to explore human behavior thoroughly. As we already established, ego and self are significantly different concepts; thus, egotism and selfishness should not be considered similar concepts in the greater scheme of semantic fields.

THE SEVENTH DISTINCTION

egotistical behaviors are first pointed out to us by others, it is usually painful and the cause of denial on our part. This phase may last one day, one year, one decade, or a lifetime. It will all depend on our personality and inner strength.

If we find enough motivation to acknowledge our egotistical behaviors, we will allow them to enter our conscious mind so we can modify them. This will gradually reduce the ego in our behavior and let our inner self shine through. This journey, once started, never ends. Furthermore, it requires the highest commitment, as its challenges tend to peak at the most inconvenient times.

The most commonly known form of egotism is arrogance, including all its synonyms (narcissism, haughtiness, pride, and the like.) Yet egotism may take many other forms, including extreme loyalty, serviceability, romanticism, shyness, and extravagance, just to name a few. An adult person's ego will always try to reutilize and optimize the relational strategies that proved successful for social adaptability during childhood and adolescence. Therefore, there are many different types of egotisms.

For example, if our parents expected us to be superior to all the other kids during our childhood, we would probably become perfectionist and judgmental adults. In turn, if our families expected us to be "good people" when we were kids, we would likely grow into serviceable, maybe even co-dependent, adults. Finally, if we were expected not to be loud and disruptive kids, we would likely become shy and introverted adults. In all such cases, we would be behaving, as adults, in response to our early conditioning for social approval. Therefore, we would be behaving in an egotistical manner.

Humility

Humility is the act of relating to others from our true self, as devoid as possible of our ego—put another way, with a well-managed ego. Humility is the capacity to recognize our strengths and weaknesses with freedom. Humility allows us to experience our achievements devoid of conceit and our failures devoid of shame. This way, our achievements and failures can help us learn more about ourselves and those around us. This is why humility is considered the highest of virtues.

Through humility, we are true to ourselves and others. Likewise, we can start to figure out all the other truths of life. In so doing, we start walking the path of wisdom and developing the remaining human virtues.

For example, by being humble, we can acknowledge our impatience, its resulting anxiety,

THE SEVENTH DISTINCTION

and the inevitability of time. In so doing, we develop patience. Likewise, by being humble, we can acknowledge our intolerance, its resulting unnecessary conflicts, and the inevitability of human differences. In so doing, we develop tolerance. Finally, by being humble, we can acknowledge the lies we have told, its resulting heartbreak, and the need for trusting relationships. In so doing, we develop sincerity. And so on.

Humility is the source of the greatest human strength. So much so, that many religious, political, and social organizations have managed to distort its meaning to make it signify the exact opposite (i.e. self-denial, subjugation, fear, and weakness.) A humble person does not cave. A humble person fights with determination while being open to learning. A humble person knows when to listen and when to speak out. A humble person does not hide, stay silent, or act against his or her own dignity.

Humility is the way of the truth, both internal and external. "The truth shall set you free," said Jesus of Nazareth. This is probably the greatest phrase ever spoken. I now read it as, "Through humility, my inner self will set me free. Free from what? Free from my ego." He also said, "Love thy neighbor as yourself." I now read that as, "Only my neighbor can set me free by showing me my inner self. How can I not love the one who sets me free? Such an act of liberation can only inspire love in return."

Modesty

Modesty is the act of relating to others through our ego with the clear objective to be judged as humble. Modesty is a particular form of egotism that surfaces whenever we know that others expect us to be humble. By this course of action, we will make sure others acknowledge our strengths and achievements without seeming conceited. Likewise, we will acknowledge our weaknesses and failures in ways that make us look virtuously humble rather than simply flawed.

In this regard, modesty can be defined as the subtlest, most sophisticated form of egotism. Depending on how we experience modesty, it can be the way to start either exploring true humility or developing the most efficient deception skills imaginable. This is when our ethical character is ultimately revealed.

The Challenge

Based on everything previously stated, I hereby propose humility as the cornerstone of personal mastery, leadership, and peak performance. Humility is the result of summoning the necessary courage to master one's inner self despite the ego's powerful

THE SEVENTH DISTINCTION

defense mechanisms. In so doing, we can help bring people together based on a shared truth. Likewise, we can use the energy previously held hostage by the ego in order to pursue our most challenging projects.

It is of paramount importance to understand that our Western culture is built largely on the paradigm of Darwinian competition, which emphasizes and exalts egos. Therefore, developing humility is nothing short of an epic challenge. It is also important not to be judgmental of others as we develop our humility. Our resolution to develop humility does not obligate others to do so. Humility is the way of pioneers who have the courage to be true to themselves and to see others as opportunities instead of threats. The question is: What kind of a person do you want to be?

REFERENCES

[1] Osho. (1977). *I Say unto You: Talks on the Sayings of Jesus* (Vol. 2, 2003 ed.). New Delhi: Diamond Pocket Books Pvt. Ltd.

[2] Whitehead, A. N. (2011). *Science and the Modern World.* New York: Cambridge University Press (Original work published in 1926).

[3] Whitman, W. (2009). *Leaves of Grass.* Nashville: American Renaissance (Original work published in 1855).

[4] Forrester, J. W. (1975). *Collected Papers of Jay W. Forrester.* Waltham, MA: Pegasus Communications.

[5] Ibid.

[6] Santayana, G. with collaboration from Smith, L. P. (1921) *Little Essays.* New York: Charles Scribner's Sons.

[7] Boole, G. (2009). *An Investigation of the Laws of Thought: On Which Are Founded the Mathematical Theories of Logic and Probabilities* (Original work published in 1854). New York: Cambridge University Press.

[8] Drucker, P. F. (2001). *The Essential Drucker.* HarperCollins Publishers, Inc.

[9] Zaleznik, A. (1977). Managers and Leaders:

Are They Different? *Harvard Business Review,* May-June, 67-78.

[10] Drucker, P. F. (1954). *The Practice of Management.* New York: Harper & Row.

[11] Ibid.

[12] Drucker, P. F. (1993). *Management: Tasks, Responsibilities, Practices.* New York: HarperCollins Publishers (Original work published in 1973).

[13] Welch, J. (2011) *Jack: Straight from the Gut.* New York: Warner Books, Inc.

[14] Rowe, D. E. and Schulmann, R. (2007) *Einstein on Politics: His Private Thoughts and Public Stands on Nationalism, Zionism, War, Peace, and the Bomb.* Princeton: Princeton University Press.

[15] Jung, C. G. (1990) *Psychological Types (A Revision by R.F.C. Hull of the Translation by H.G. Baynes).* Princeton: Princeton University Press (Original work published in 1923).

[16] Harper, D. (2012). *Online Etymology Dictionary.* Retrieved from http://www.etymonline.com/index.php?term=ambition&allowed_in_frame=0 (accessed December 5, 2012)

[17] Harper, D. (2012). *Online Etymology Dictionary.* Retrieved from

References

http://www.etymonline.com/index.php?term=mission&allowed_in_frame=0 (accessed December 5, 2012)

[18] Maxwell, J. C. (2007). *The 21 Irrefutable Laws of Leadership*. Nashville, TN: Thomas Nelson Inc.

[19] Ibid.

[20] Harper, D. (2012). *Online Etymology Dictionary*. Retrieved from http://www.etymonline.com/index.php?term=vision&allowed_in_frame=0 (accessed December 5, 2012)

[21] Ibid.

[22] Osho. (2001). *Awareness: The Key to Living in Balance* (Rev. ed.). New York: St. Martin's Press.

[23] Santayana, G. (2012). *The Life of Reason or the Phases of Human Progress* (Rev. ed., Vol. 1). Forgotten Books (Original work published in 1906).

[24] Lincoln, A. (1858, June 16). *A House Divided: Acceptance Speech at the Illinois Republican Party's Nomination for the US Senate.* Retrieved from http://www.nationalcenter.org/HouseDivided.html (accessed December 5, 2012)

[25] Kant, I. (2007) *Kant: Groundwork of the Metaphysics of Morals (Translated by Thomas*

THE SEVENTH DISTINCTION

Kingsmill Abbott). RadaClassic.com (Original work published in 1785).

INDEX

Ambition .. *8*, *55*, *57*, *64*
Boole, George *21*
Competency *45*, *46*
Complexity . 12, 13, 20, 47, 51, 61
Complication.. 8, *11*, *13*
Consciousness
  Conscious... 8, 47, 75, 82
Conviction 8, 67
Drucker, Peter F. *33*, *38*
Ego 2, 4, 5, 6, 47, 49, 56, 58, 59, 62, 69, 75, 76, 77, 78, 79, 80, 81, 82, 83, 84, 85, 86, 87, 88
Einstein, Albert ... 6, 45, 80
Evolution.. 8, *19*, *31*, *45*
Forrester, Jay *17*
Influence .. 8, *33*, *34*, *37*
Jesus of Nazareth 6, *60*, 75, *86*
Jung, Carl G. 50, 51, 52, 55
Kant, Immanuel 67
Leadership... 33, 34, 36, 37, 38, 39, 40, 41, 42, 43, 49, 61, 71, 76, 83, 87
Learning *18*, *19*, *24*, *25*, 86
Lincoln, Abraham.... 64
Management . 8, *17*, *33*, 34, 35, 36, 38
Maxwell, John C. 59
Mission 8, 55, 59, 64
Obligation 8, 67
Osho 6
Performance . 5, *12*, *18*, 24, *33*, 35, *46*, 53, 76, 87
Personal mastery .. 4, 5, 70, 76, 79, 83, 87
Personality
  Personality type(s)
    Personality model(s) .. 36, 45, 46, 47, 48, 49, 50, 53, 70
Principle
  Principled 8, 67
Santayana, George.. *19*, 64
Self ... 3, 4, 6, 11, 22, 24, 27, 28, 29, 30, 39, 47,

THE SEVENTH DISTINCTION

51, 55, 58, 59, 60, 67, 68, 69, 70, 75, 76, 77, 79, 80, 81, 82, 83, 84, 86, 87

Simplicity.... *11, 12, 17, 18, 20*

Systems thinking. *6, 15, 19*

Talent *8, 45, 46*

Understanding *8, 19, 20, 21, 22, 23, 28, 30*

Vision *55, 61*

Welch, Jack *39, 40*

Whitehead, Alfred N. *8*

Whitman, Walt *11*

www.ingramcontent.com/pod-product-compliance
Lightning Source LLC
LaVergne TN
LVHW041633070426
835507LV00008B/596